EVERYDAY FAITH

APPLYING THE SERMON ON THE MOUNT TO THE WORKPLACE

Don Latham

Terra Nova Publications

First published by Terra Nova Publications Ltd, 2001

ISBN 1 901949 10 9

*Published in Great Britain by
Terra Nova Publications Ltd
PO Box 2400, Bradford on Avon, Wiltshire BA15 2YN*

*Cover design: Gazelle Creative Productions
Cover printed by The Shires Press, Trowbridge, Wiltshire*

*Printed in Great Britain at
The Cromwell Press, Trowbridge, Wiltshire*

CONTENTS

1. THE BEATITUDES

Matthew 5:1–12

The standards that Jesus teaches in the Sermon on the Mount cover a great many aspects of our lives: attitudes to money, ethics, spirituality, practicalities of living, and the way we relate to others. One of the greatest challenges to the Christian is how we live out our faith every day. Faith for every day is intensely practical as we put into operation the things Jesus teaches. He taught a pattern of living which is often in marked contrast to the standards of the world in which we live and work. John Stott has aptly described the Sermon on the Mount as the 'most complete delineation anywhere in the New Testament of the Christian counter culture.' We are to consider the challenges of **how we apply the Sermon on the Mount to the workplace.**

Jesus taught His disciples of a present and a future kingdom. They were to be citizens of the kingdom, as we are if we have received Jesus by His Spirit into our lives. The Sermon is for all His followers, and describes the conduct He expects of us, until He returns to set up His kingdom here on earth.

The principles of the Sermon on the Mount, and in particular the Beatitudes, are benchmarks. They may seem impossible to attain. When you face an enormous task, like eating an elephant, it seems impossible. The answer is to break it down into meal size portions; it is then achievable, but takes time, persistence, patience and endurance. The Christian life is like running a long distance race—when we often want it to be a sprint! Jesus breaks down the teaching into meal size portions.

Remember that Jesus was young, and that He was surrounded by a group of ordinary, young, largely uneducated men. He gave this teaching at the beginning of His public ministry, having not long had the experience of being baptised by John in the River Jordan and subsequently spending time in the desert. The Beatitudes are like a table of contents or context for the Sermon, providing, as Jeff Lucas would say, a 'helicoptic view'.

Nine times Jesus declares us to be blessed. I love it when a golfer wins a tournament and at the post match interview says he is blessed. You know immediately he is a Christian! The Greek word for 'blessed' is *makarios,* which means happy or jubilant.

Blessed are the poor in spirit,
For theirs is the kingdom of heaven.

(v. 3)

Being 'poor in spirit' means that we are living thankful lives, appreciative of God's gifts to us, which releases us to be outward looking and able to express His love and compassion for others. It also means that we are good stewards of our possessions for the Lord's use in His kingdom. Trying to fulfil the teaching of the Sermon on the Mount will not make us righteous—only Christ can do that. Righteousness is a free gift—that only costs our lives to receive. If we have not entered the kingdom, and blessings that go with it, that is our choice.

Blessed are those who mourn,
For they shall be comforted.

(v. 4)

In human terms, mourning is not seen as a state of 'blessedness' or happiness. But when the Holy Spirit comes, even the bleakest situation can be transformed.

I remember praying in a village church in Somerset for a girl in some distress. It was late and I wanted to get home. 'What is the problem?' I asked her friend. It was then explained to me that her husband of one week had drowned in a canoeing accident. I joined in the tears and prayed with her to receive Jesus and the power of the kingdom—the Holy Spirit. He is the Comforter and she found comfort and strength in Him as she rebuilt her life following her tragic loss. The colleague who loses a young son in a car accident, the mother who loses a baby; there is no shortage of opportunity to bring the comfort of the Holy Spirit into the workplace.

Blessed are the meek.
For they shall inherit the earth.

(v. 5)

Sadly, meekness has been associated with weakness. The word 'meek' means teachable. We are to, 'Receive with meekness the implanted word' (James 1:21). If we stay teachable, we inherit the earth. One thing that surprises me is how little Christians read.

At work, why is it necessary to go for a policy of promoting young people? Is it sometimes because older generations have not remained teachable? Change is the order of the day in the workplace. There is new revelation and new understanding to be gained, and there are great challenges today. As a Christian, do I display the characteristic of being teachable—or am I set in my ways?

Blessed are those who hunger and thirst for righteousness,
For they shall be filled.

(v. 6)

We can do without food and water for a short time, but in order to grow we need a fresh supply every day. We need to work daily at our fellowship with God. As we read His Word and pray, it creates in us a hunger for more.

As I listened to one of the leaders in the Argentine revival, I learnt the important lesson that if we want to see the power of God demonstrated in our place of work then there must not be things in our lives that would offend the Holy Spirit. We face the challenge of being holy in an unholy and sometimes hostile environment. It does take discipline to make time during our working day for fellowship with God, but the promise is 'they shall be filled.'

Blessed are the merciful,
For they shall obtain mercy.

(v. 7)

Grace is unmerited and undeserved. Mercy is grace in action and should characterise our behaviour at work. Do we show mercy in all our business relationships? If we know God's forgiveness, then we will forgive. We cannot afford not to forgive.

Notice that Jesus' words carry an uncomfortable implication, that it is the merciful who obtain mercy. So we must not be amongst the unmerciful! We all need God's mercy; it is indispensable! So to be merciful in thought, speech and action is not merely a good suggestion, it is essential if we are to please God. Mercy and forgiveness should enable us to resolve disputes and misunderstanding.

Blessed are the pure in heart,
For they shall see God.

(v. 8)

To remain pure in heart, we need to examine ourselves. Psalm 66 says, *If I regard iniquity in my heart the Lord will not hear* (v. 18). When we remain pure in heart, we begin to be more and more aware of the true character of God. This is essential if we are to take His kingdom into our workplaces. There has to be an end to the sacred/secular divide.

In Chapter seven we consider the importance of forgiveness in prayer. For now we note that one result of that purity in heart which Jesus requires of us is a willingness to release forgiveness to others.

Blessed are the peacemakers,
For they shall be called sons of God.

(v. 9)

We have a ministry of reconciliation. The workplace provides a wonderful opportunity for effective Christian witness. Witnessing is letting others know by our lives and words that we are children of God. It should be natural, spontaneous and built on the solid foundation of putting the Sermon on the Mount into practice in our everyday lives. **This is true everyday faith.**

Blessed are those who are persecuted for righteousness' sake,
For theirs is the kingdom of heaven.

Blessed are you when they revile and persecute you, and say all kinds of evil against you falsely for My sake.

(vv. 10–11)

The Sermon is about going on to maturity. The workplace is not a soft option for the Christian and it does not necessarily become any easier as you reach more responsible and senior levels. I have known what it is like to come through difficult situations with a positive outcome but also the loss of a contract in a way I considered unjust. In all such situations, where we have stood for what is right and received unfair treatment we can rejoice!

...for great is your reward in heaven.

(v. 12)

We must keep a kingdom perspective on our daily pressures at work. It will be hard at times, but we look for heavenly rewards. This is something far greater than any annual performance appraisal or City bonus can offer.

2. *BEING SALT AND LIGHT*

Matthew 5:13–16

Twin Christian characteristics which we have to demonstrate in the workplace are being 'salt' and 'light'. When we acknowledge Jesus Christ to be the Son of God, ask forgiveness for our sin and invite Him into our lives, He comes by the power of the Holy Spirit and creates a *new* spirit within us that is perfect—righteous. By the action of God we are spiritually re-born and brought into relationship with Him—and we become members of the kingdom. This is the only way to obtain membership. The new spirit in us is like salt—and should affect *everything* we say and do.

I once spoke at a well-known agricultural college on the topic of healing. The Chaplain wanted an academic talk, but I forgot to tell God it was academic, and there were a number of wonderful healings. More importantly, a number of students became Christians. It was all so amazing that word got around the college and I was asked to go back a few days later, to give another talk. Being taken to the venue by car, one of the students who had become a Christian said, "Don, since Monday I have not had the same physical relationship with my boyfriend. I just know it is wrong." No one had told her, other than the Spirit of God within her. Contrast this with a church I was at a few weeks ago, praying with people at the end of the service. A tearful young woman asked me to pray for a boyfriend she could trust. My reaction was to say, "That is fine; we will pray for a Christian boyfriend."

Her response shook me. She said, "That is the problem; they are the ones who want me to sleep with them." Why the difference? Sin, which in this case was sex outside marriage, will cause a break in fellowship, but not our relationship, with God.

You are the salt of the earth; but if the salt loses its flavor, how shall it be seasoned? It is then good for nothing but to be thrown out and trampled underfoot by men (Matt. 5:13).

Salt is a preservative and our Christian lives should preserve the good. Salt brings out the flavour in that which may otherwise be bland. If we do not retain our distinctiveness, what use are we? Our Christian witness gets trampled under foot. I address such issues in *Being Unmistakably Christian at Work* (Terra Nova). We lose our salty taste by the process of 'gradualism'. Because we are often in a minority, especially in the workplace, we gradually take on the standards of the people around us. Instead of being a blessing to others, our lives become bland and we sound like and behave like non-Christians. I like the illustration of the frog. If you put it in hot water it will jump out. But if you put it in cold water and boil it up, it will sit there until it boils to death.

If we are to act as salt, then we must remain in fellowship with God. Salt is a type of the word of God, and for our lives to be like a salt shaker we must constantly refresh the supply of salt by finding time in our busy lifestyles for the Word of God. *Walk in wisdom toward those who are outside, redeeming the time. Let your speech always be with grace, seasoned with salt, that you may know how you ought to answer each one* (Col. 4:5–6). We do not have to try to be salt; our lives will be like salt if we maintain our fellowship with God. *If we confess our sins, He is faithful and just to forgive us our sins and to cleanse us from all unrighteousness* (1 John 1:9).

You are the light of the world. A city that is set on a hill cannot be hidden (Matt. 5:14).

We are called to be in the world—but not of it. The workplace is a place of God's calling where we are to demonstrate the fruit of the Spirit and the power of the Spirit in our lives. There is no hiding place, and we should not be hidden. Having lived in an area for a long time, we are a well-known Christian family. It is a challenge when the book on your life (*A Faith that Works*) is sold in Tesco, in the village and in other secular book shops, and read with interest by your work colleagues. It means that I cannot have a day off to be miserable—I have to be constantly joyful! Seriously, people will look at our lives on Monday morning; when we are under pressure; when things may seem to have gone wrong, and they will watch our reactions. We are exposed, 'set on a hill', and that is the great challenge for Christians at work.

Let your light so shine before men, that they may see your good works and glorify your Father in heaven (Matt. 5:16).

Light exposes, illuminates, and dispels gloom. Our effective witness at work is, I believe, 90% about lifestyle and 10% about what we say. We do need to be able to articulate our faith, but it is our good works that will get attention and will glorify God. These good works do not always have to be 'spectacular' and it is often the simplest things that make the impact. I learnt so much from working with a highly respected Christian Chief Executive. His concern for all staff and their families was evident in all that he said and did. His witness was warm and uncompromising. He would regularly lunch with a group of staff to 'keep in touch' and later I did the same. When my staff were facing a weekend at work in order to get a new system in place by the required date, I joined them and made them tea and coffee. As Chief Executive I may have lacked the technical skills, but at least I could serve them and show appreciation. It is what my mentor would have done. We need to provoke each other to do good works—and the right mentor can assist.

Are we being salt and light, and doing good works that glorify God?

3. HAVE THE RIGHT ATTITUDE

Matthew 5:17–32

When we think about sin, we tend to think of the outward action; but consider a list of seven sins that God says He hates:

These six things the LORD hates,
Yes, seven are an abomination to Him:
A proud look,
A lying tongue,
Hands that shed innocent blood,
A heart that devises wicked plans,
Feet that are swift in running to evil,
A false witness who speaks lies,
And one who sows discord among brethren.

Prov. 6:16–19

Note the emphasis there on sins of thought or speech, and in Matt. 5:22 we read:

But I say to you that whoever is angry with his brother without a cause shall be in danger of the judgment. And whoever says to his brother, 'Raca!' shall be in danger of the council. But whoever says, 'You fool!' shall be in danger of hell fire.

Clearly, God is going to judge thoughts in the same way He judges deeds. The Pharisees practised an outward righteousness, but for the Christian there is to be an inner righteousness—from the heart.

Christians must demonstrate a Spirit-controlled temperament. *Raca* stands for words that offend men, and anger is the emotion that releases them. To judge a man spiritually by calling him a fool is passing a judgment that belongs only to God. (See Chapter ten.)

Therefore if you bring your gift to the altar, and there remember that your brother has something against you, leave your gift there before the altar, and go your way. First be reconciled to your brother, and then come and offer your gift (Matt. 5:23–24).

This is the important principle: that we must judge ourselves before we do anything. If we are not pure in heart, our prayers are ineffective. Forgiveness is at the heart of all that Jesus teaches on prayer. Have we wronged another person? We have 'The Peace' before communion, not simply as a test for those who find personal contact difficult, but to put right those differences. We need to do the same at work.

We should seek ways of reaching agreement without compromising what we believe, for: *If it is possible, as much as depends on you, live peaceably with all men* (Romans 12:18). It is possible to hold differences of view without being argumentative or offensive. I always wanted a management team and not a management 'club'; a place where Directors could openly share different views and experience—especially if they differed from mine. Our combined experience and wisdom was greater than that of any individual.

Relationships at work are an opportunity for friendship, witness—and problems! I love people, working in a team, and being a leader. My first senior management role was achieved at the age of twenty-nine, when I became Assistant Director of Social Services for Wiltshire County Council. Managing a large number of staff, many of whom were older than me, and the majority women, was a challenge—and I had much to learn. Relationships in the office can be a minefield, and as Christians we must be impeccable in our words and actions. We should always act professionally, with prudence, using effective communications. Our speech and language should edify the listener. We should treat others in the way we would wish to be treated ourselves.

As employers, we should determine patterns of work that provide rest, safety, productivity and effectiveness. We should give appropriate time to training and personal development; establish personnel policies which offer each employee the maximum opportunity to work productively and ethically, and to grow to full potential; have policies that offer equal opportunities for men and women, which respect the dignity of each individual; and make management decisions in the light of personal, marriage and family needs.

I must admit to having been naïve about issues of harassment and discrimination, until I had responsibilities for Equal Opportunities, as an Assistant Chief Executive. I was rapidly educated by the council's expert, and gained valuable experience in dealing with such issues. It is not difficult to promote women to positions they merit, but much more difficult to handle issues of sexual harassment or discrimination against minority groups. We must keep right relationships, encourage reconciliation, be positive, and do what is righteous.

4. KEEP YOUR WORD

Matthew 5:33–37

But let your 'Yes' be 'Yes,' and your 'No,' 'No.' For whatever is more than this is from the evil one (Matt. 5:37).

Jesus forbids oaths but, as has rightly been pointed out, we must beware of falling into the same trap as the Pharisees. They failed to see that what lay behind the commands was the need for honesty, truthfulness and reliability. Jesus' words illuminate the spirit and intention behind the Old Testament Law. At the heart of Jesus' teaching is the key principle that we should keep our word—this is to be a mark of Christian character. Jesus said, *"I am the ...truth,"* (John 14:6). So as Christians we should be truthful and trustworthy in our homes, personal relationships and work.

In a world that uses oaths to ensure that people tell the truth, we must have an inward truthfulness that does not depend on oaths. When we give our 'yes', it is to be 'yes'; and when we give our 'no', it is to be 'no'. Men and women who are of truthful character will be truthful, whether or not they are under oath. We should never have to add, 'Now I am telling you the truth,' or 'as God is my witness.' The high priest, when addressing Jesus, trying to elicit a response to his question, said, "I put you under oath by the living God.... Tell us if you are the Christ, the Son of God!"

Jesus did *not* then swear in the name of God His Father, but simply answered, "It is as you said..." (Matthew 26:63-64). It is sometimes suggested that Paul, in effect, put himself under oath on two occasions, to emphasise the importance of what he was saying, but in neither of them does he swear by God or His name. (See 2 Corinthians 1:23 and Galatians 1:20). What Paul is doing is reminding his readers that what he says is said in the presence of God. This, surely, is a salutary reminder to us that what we say as Christians is said in the presence of God. All we say and do, and every affirmation we make, is heard by Him. What an awesome truth!

For some Christians the avoidance of oath-taking is a matter of the highest principle, so it is a good thing that, according to English law, a form of affirmation may be used instead of the oaths usually sworn in God's name (e.g. in law courts.)

Clearly, the heart of the matter Jesus was talking about was whether or not we are truthful. God's word to us is always 'yes' or 'no', and others should be able to depend on our 'yes' and 'no'. *For all the promises of God in Him are Yes, and in Him Amen, to the glory of God through us* (2 Corinthians 1:20).

This is one of the greatest challenges to us as Christians in the workplace. I can speak from personal experience that to act with integrity can put your job and career at risk, and I have to admit that challenging Christians to be honest at work has resulted in some losing jobs. A few years ago I gave a public lecture at Bath University entitled, 'Can you be honest and successful?' It was so popular that they had to do a third reprint of the talk: clearly this is an issue that stimulates many people, leading them to reflect on vital principles. Giving the same talk to the sixth form of Bristol Grammar School generated an excellent debate. There, one pupil openly challenged me with the question: "Aren't you an anachronism—to believe that you can be honest and successful today?" An audience of businessmen in Buenos Aires was equally amazed at the concept.

One cannot have integrity without being honest, but one can certainly be honest and yet at the same time have little integrity. Integrity requires three steps: discerning what is wrong; acting on what you have discerned, even at personal cost; and saying openly that you are acting on your understanding of what is right and wrong. The first step requires moral and spiritual awareness. The second brings in the ideal of a person of integrity as being steadfast—a quality that includes keeping one's commitments. The third reminds us that a person of integrity can be trusted.

Concerning the difference between honesty and integrity, it is important to understand that a person may be entirely honest without ever engaging in the hard work of discernment. You do not have to tell people everything you know. Lying and non-disclosure, as the law often recognises, are not the same thing. Sometimes, it is actually illegal to tell what you know, as for example, in the disclosure of certain financial information by market insiders. Or it may be unethical, as when a lawyer reveals a confidence entrusted to her by a client. It may be simple bad manners. Telling everything may harm someone else (i.e. being 'brutally' honest). If forthrightness is not preceded by discernment, it may result in the expression of a wrong moral judgment and it can be used to escape duties and responsibilities. We need honesty and integrity combined, and we need to work it out day by day in our own workplace. In this way we can encourage a culture of trust, openness and honesty. We can choose whether we speak honest, life-filled words or destructive negative words. Jesus said: *The words that I speak to you are spirit, and they are life* (John 6 :63b). Words are powerful: *Death and life are in the power of the tongue, and those who love it will eat its fruit* (Prov. 18:21). *A good man shall eat good from the fruit of his mouth.... He who guards his mouth keeps his life, but he who opens wide his lips will come to ruin* [AMP] (Prov. 13:2–3). We must keep our promises, be honest, think before we speak and say 'sorry' when we fail.

5. *GO THE SECOND MILE*

Matthew 5:38–48

Should Christians retaliate *(an eye for an eye and a tooth for a tooth)* or should we not resist an evil person? (See v. 39.) When Jesus spoke, I do not believe He was addressing the general situation, where a Christian can rightly use the law (cp. Romans 13) for protection or restitution. The circumstances being addressed are those which apply when we are being persecuted for the sake of righteousness. We need to look at this injunction in the light of the whole Sermon. Remember these beatitudes: *Blessed are those who are persecuted for righteousness' sake, For theirs is the kingdom of heaven. Blessed are you when they revile and persecute you, and say all kinds of evil against you falsely for My sake* (Matt. 5:10–11). Clearly, Jesus was talking about our stand for the gospel. He is not saying we should be weak and feeble, allowing ourselves to be robbed and cheated. It is rather that, when we are suffering for His sake, for the kingdom of God, then we are neither to resort to the law nor retaliate in kind. *Beloved, do not avenge yourselves, but rather give place to wrath; for it is written, "Vengeance is Mine, I will repay," says the Lord* (Romans 12:19).

Courts are not the way to settle things between Christians (see 1 Cor. 6:1–8) and some Christians think we should never go to court for any reason. But here Jesus is talking about going to court because of the gospel: *If anyone wants to sue you and take away your tunic, let him have your cloak also* (v. 40).

'This verse is not referring to natural cases but to being sued for the gospel's sake, for righteousness' sake.' —Bob Yandian.[1]

It is in these circumstances we may 'give our cloak also' in order to get things settled without recourse to a court battle. It is a matter of great sadness, and does great harm to the kingdom of God, when Christians feud in public. We may know of workplace disputes between Christians. We should pray, and seek reconciliation. There are Christians skilled in arbitration who can be called upon to assist. If we do suffer injustice, God really can redeem and restore our situation.

Under Roman law, a soldier could compel a Jew to carry his pack for a mile. This was often done with much complaining. Jesus teaches not only that you do not complain, but go the second mile. The simple lesson here is that for the first mile you have an obligation toward him, but for the second mile he is obligated to you. As Christians, we have to 'earn' the right to share our faith. Going the second mile is one way to achieve that position. Recently, when I was working alongside another Christian accountant, we suddenly lost half the financial team. Thanks to my young colleague's skill and application, the work was not only maintained but many problems were resolved. The Director of HR was so impressed she asked him out for lunch, because she wanted to know what motivated him. Going the second mile provided the opportunity for testimony, which I was later happy to build on. We may need to give or lend—which, again, is part of our witness. This needs wisdom, as our families are our first responsibility. Nevertheless, generosity is a characteristic which marks out the people of God, and we need to demonstrate this at work.

But I say to you, love your enemies, bless those who curse you, do good to those who hate you, and pray for those who spitefully use you and persecute you (Matt 5:44). Who said the Christian life was easy! This is how we are to show our maturity and our sonship. *Therefore you shall be perfect, just as your Father in heaven is perfect* (Matt. 5:48).

We may experience all these things in our place of work, and the sign of our maturity will be how we respond. Is this possible, and does it work? All my experience says 'yes'—even when my mind and emotions are saying 'no, it's unfair.' In one job (which I had no doubt was God's appointment) I went through a time, following a change of leadership, when no matter what I did it seemed impossible to please—and I parted company with that organization. I felt unjustly treated, but I made the decision not to hold it against them. As a result, I am free; I have spoken blessings over them. Why it happened I still do not know; it may have been part of my maturity programme.

A councillor was being particularly difficult and critical in public meetings. I told my wife of the problems he was causing, and she said, 'Isn't that good; it is a chance to start praying for him and speaking God's blessing over him.' I had wanted to throttle him! But, like R.T. Kendall, I have learnt one of the basic rules for success: listen to your wife. We started to pray for, and bless, that councillor. The transformation was dramatic. He quickly became so positive and supportive. Speaking on the topic of praise, at a parish weekend in Devon, I was convicted about my attitude to a difficult member of the public, whose problem I had inherited. Despite my efforts to resolve the problem, it troubled me even more. That weekend, I praised and spoke God's blessing over the person concerned. Within three days there was a remarkable resolution to what had become an intractable problem. We reached a settlement which, when reported to Council, caused delight at the outcome—and I got the credit!

Sometimes I say that I can quickly locate where a person is on their walk with God once I hear them speak. The word of God works, and the mature Christian is the one who believes it, speaks it and, most importantly, acts upon it.

[1] in *Salt and Light*, published by Harrison House

6. DO GOOD TO PLEASE GOD

Matthew 6:1–4

Take heed that you do not do your charitable deeds before men, to be seen by them. Otherwise you have no reward from your Father in heaven (Matt. 6:1).

It follows from this statement that charitable deeds are expected of us, and that they give pleasure to God. Moreover, as long as we do not display them before men we will get a reward from God in this life, for, ... *your Father who sees in secret will reward you openly* (v. 4b) —And for eternity! How important it is to keep a kingdom perspective on life. What are the charitable deeds we can do in the workplace? These are things over and above what should be expected of us in doing our work with excellence. There are always opportunities: to show concern, give practical assistance, and listen. Often, the most precious thing we have is time, and the best thing we can give to people is our attention. For me, this was often a chat in the early morning or over lunch, and followed up by prayer. Colleagues would call in to see me at a point of crisis such as an accident in the family, the break-up of a relationship, or for advice on practical financial problems, redundancy or sickness. These charitable deeds were not done at a cost to my employer. They were done privately, but sometimes became known, because of significant answers to prayer.

We are not alone in doing charitable deeds, for non-Christians do them also, and often better. However, for us they are not optional, but are integral to effective witness. The message of the kingdom of God is for the whole person: body, soul and spirit. Our approach has to be holistic, and compassion will motivate us to do what is right. We have different gifts and skills, and we should expect God to use us in different ways. In one department in which I worked, a member of staff had a disability which could at times be distressing. I was always deeply impressed by how this was handled sensitively by a group of work colleagues who would willingly cover for him. I can think of another business that gave away 10% of its profits through a charitable trust, and the staff set up their own fund to meet the needs of the local community.

We will be involved in charitable works outside the workplace, which may or may not be church based. Mercy and the practical gift of 'helps' are regularly in action in some peoples lives, but are often unseen because of the principle enunciated by Jesus in this section of the Sermon. We are going to be surprised at the size of some of the 'mansions' in heaven!

As well as financial giving, our anointed management skills can make mission more effective, and may be the only opportunity for reaching communities that cannot be reached by the traditional missionary. We recently met a couple in central Asia who had gone out with the intention of pastoring a church. It did not work out, so the man asked God why. God told him that He had not intended him to become a pastor, but his calling was to business. Since he set up a business the work has flourished. We saw this on a visit to India last year. It was one of the most wonderful experiences of our lives. In three days of ministry we saw many saved, baptised in the Spirit and healed. An early-retired Christian businessman friend is not only putting in money but also his business experience, to encourage self-sufficiency. A combination of business skills, finance and mission are impacting on a whole region—and people are turning to Christ there in great numbers.

Businessmen are skilled at getting people to work collectively for a common purpose. We can use those skills to bring together agencies and organisations for mission. What are the good works we are called and anointed to do? For me, it has been, in particular, praying for the sick and standing by others facing dramatic change, and mentoring. Peter Gammons says: 'Success is doing well what God has called you to do.'

7. THE IMPORTANCE OF PRAYER

Matthew 6:5–14

Jesus had to *teach* His disciples how to pray. Healing and teaching they saw and heard, but praying to the Father was done privately. In this well known passage, Jesus teaches them to find a 'secret place' to pray, tells them not to use vain repetition, and suggests a model prayer. We are to pray to the Father in the name of Jesus. Firstly, we are to recognise who God is and pray for His kingdom to come. Next, we are to pray for His will to be done in our lives, before we bring our daily needs to Him. We then pray for our forgiveness, which we receive in the measure we are prepared to forgive others. We can then pray for victory over temptation and for a way through difficult and even evil situations, remembering in all things to give God the glory.

The Lord's Prayer is a great framework for prayer to start the day! 'Work Zone' sessions at *Spring Harvest 1999* (Minehead) revealed that for many people the only 'secret place' was in the car, driving to work. Now I am all for increasing the effective use of time, and can recount significant encounters with God in the car; however, if we are to get the best out of the day we must give God the best we have, I suggest we need to find another place of quiet during the day, as well. To start the day early in the office was important for me. The 'in-tray' was always a challenge, and I had often to fight the temptation of starting to work before giving the day to God. Nevertheless, praising God in the car on the way to work was a good preparation.

Speak out God's attributes; praise and thank Him! Sing out loud, despite the strange looks you may get at the traffic lights! (I would recommend a different approach on the 'tube'.) One way to avoid repetition is to sing and/or pray in the Spirit (tongues). Often, we run out of English, and by using our God-given tongue we can experience freshness in our praise and prayer—and know, too, that we are being edified.

As we give the day to God, we can seek His direction and wisdom. We do not have to be someone special to get our prayers answered. *The effective, fervent prayer of a righteous man avails much. Elijah was a man with a nature like ours, and he prayed earnestly that it would not rain; and it did not rain on the land for three years and six months. And he prayed again, and the heaven gave rain, and the earth produced its fruit (James 5:16b–18).* Elijah was a man like us. I am reminded of a teacher in our home group, many years ago, who had been teaching his children that God answers prayer. They were excited, and prayed for a fine day for their school trip on a pleasure boat. The forecast for the day was rain, but he recounted with great excitement that throughout the day there had been heavy rain clouds on both sides of the boat and that they had sailed in a shaft of sunlight all day, with no rain.

For our prayers to be effective at work, we must know that we are 'called' to the workplace. With that calling we have been given authority. As we pray to the Father in the name of Jesus, we have simply to believe: *Therefore I say to you, whatever things you ask when you pray, believe that you receive them, and you will have them* (Mark 11:24). We do need to be specific: *If you abide in Me, and My words abide in you, you will ask what you desire, and it shall be done for you* (John 15:7). We need to ask according to God's will: *Now this is the confidence that we have in Him, that if we ask anything according to His will* [i.e. in line with His word] *He hears us. And if we know that He hears us, whatever we ask, we know that we have the petitions that we have asked of Him* (1 John 5: 14 –15). We need to ask boldly: *Therefore, brethren, having boldness to enter the Holiest by the blood of Jesus.... Let us hold fast the confession of our hope without wavering, for He who promised is faithful* (Heb. 10: 19, 23).

There are many things that can hinder our effective prayer life at work, among them: doubting, unforgiveness, unconfessed sin, strife in marriage, wrong motives, selfishness, lack of praise and thankfulness, worry, weariness (giving up), and pride. But as we put God and His kingdom first in our lives, His desires become our desires and we will know His direction. We should pray for our employers, and for those in authority. Most often, the culture of an organisation is set by those at the top, and we must appreciate that our prayers can make a difference. When I was Chief Executive of a local authority, we achieved a corporate plan endorsed by all forty three members of a politically diverse council. It was a well presented and negotiated plan, but it was also, as far as I was concerned, a matter of much prayer.

We should pray for our friends and colleagues at work. They have the same pressures and challenges that we face, but without Christ they do not have the same 'invisible' means of support. I have discovered that once you start praying for individuals, things start to happen. One key area for me has been to pray for those who are sick. I can recount many stories of healing, often leading to the individuals coming to know Christ for themselves. If we are to see the kingdom of God in the workplace, prayer is essential. God will show us who to pray for and how to pray.

Jesus said, *when you fast...* (Matt. 6:16). The implication is that fasting does have its place for us today, and Jesus again teaches that this is to be done in 'secret'. This is not easy when you are working and the working or business lunch is part of your work style—there may even be the *Alpha* supper! But, in my experience, if God calls you to fast for a purpose, then there will always be a reward. I have seen this to be true in the areas of receiving direction, revelation, a release of spiritual gifts and breakthrough in difficult situations, not least in the workplace.

A requirement of the personal fast is that all strife, gossip, backbiting, and every form of false, unjust or unkind speaking must be put away. The believer must be operating in the love of God. Fasting allows our spirit to dominate the flesh. It does not change God, but it changes us, and He can give us the desires of our heart.

8. LAY UP TREASURES IN HEAVEN

Matthew 6:19–24

Jesus teaches a great deal about possessions, money and giving. In these verses, He is speaking of earthly riches but is *not* teaching that possessions and prosperity are evil. Rather, He is talking about the purpose of our lives: being single-minded about putting God first, and not storing up goods because of fear. The danger is that mammon (the Chaldean god of money) takes over control, becoming our focus. In the Christian life, money is not in itself wrong, and we should expect proper recompense at work. Money as such is neither good nor evil; only the love of money is evil. *For the love of money is a root of all kinds of evil...* (1 Tim. 6:10). If we focus our eyes on money, we can lose everything. If we set our eyes on the Lord, to serve Him alone, then money will be there to meet our every need.

Jesus is not saying that you should withdraw from business activity but, rather, do not rely on or trust in riches. The key to God's prosperity is to put Him first. How can we do this in our finances? —by tithing. Giving the first 10% of our income to God is the most practical way of demonstrating that He comes first.

The tithe was in existence before the Law of Moses, and is therefore a principle which is still relevant under the New Covenant —although we are no longer under the Law. It is meant to be from the first fruits of our income (Neh. 10:35) and it should not be calculated on what we have left. (See Prov. 3:9.) Tithing is not a gift (See Mal. 3:8.) It belongs to God, and a priority for it should be the place we receive spiritual food.

"Will a man rob God?
Yet you have robbed Me!
But you say, 'In what way have we robbed You?'
In tithes and offerings.
You are cursed with a curse,

For you have robbed Me,
Even this whole nation.
Bring all the tithes into the storehouse,
That there may be food in my house, And try Me now in this,"
Says the LORD of hosts,
"If I will not open for you the windows of heaven
And pour out for you such blessing
That there will not be room enough to receive it.
"And I will rebuke the devourer for your sakes...."

(Mal. 3:8–11)

God promises a blessing bigger than we will know what to do with: to rebuke the devourer on our behalf, and His blessing will be so evidently upon us that people will call us happy and blessed. We cannot afford not to tithe. John Wesley said that one of the greatest sins in the Church was 'mental assent' —in other words, agreeing with the word of God without putting it into practice. Tithing is a foundation for individual and corporate blessing and growth. We need to reassess our tithe every time we get a change in our income. If we run our own business, then we should be tithing our profits.

All our giving must be out of love and should be directed by the Holy Spirit. Over and above our tithe we can give to the poor and, most importantly, give to 'the gospel.' As I travel more and more, it is evident that one of the things which most holds back the extension of God's kingdom is the lack of financial resources. I believe that God wants to bless financially those in business, so that they can be a resource for His kingdom. A few months ago, I visited a church where a young businessman had determined that he did not need to improve his own living standard and was ploughing his increased income into Christian work. His view was that a millionaire is someone who has given away a million pounds. No wonder his business is being blessed!

The lamp of the body is the eye. If therefore your eye is good, your whole body will be full of light (Matt. 6:22).
Light comes through the eye, and the brain interprets what we see. The 'eye' here speaks of the mind, or thoughts, which takes me back to my first point that we need to be single-minded, with our mind on the Lord. It is a challenge to do this with all the pressures and distractions of work. The alternative is a bad eye (see v.23) which is double-mindedness. This results in *being unstable in all* [our] *ways* (James 1:8) and, consequently, in danger of being deceived.

No man can serve two masters; for either he will hate the one and love the other, or else he will be loyal to the one and despise the other. You cannot serve God and mammon (Matt. 6:24)
The key to success is to be single-minded in serving the Lord.

9. DO NOT WORRY

Matthew 6:25–34

Three times in this passage, Jesus instructs us not to worry. With deadlines to meet, a lack of resources, suppliers who do not supply, debtors who do not pay—Jesus nonetheless says to you: 'do not worry'! If we can learn to put this into practice, we shall have a distinctive Christian witness in the workplace. A secretary once said to me, 'I could not understand how you carried the pressure (for a few months I had been working from early in the morning until late at night) and why you did not seem to worry.' This was one of the times I put into practice what I teach others! A few months later she became a Christian—and it was not because of what I *said*. We have to make a lifestyle decision not to worry. One of my memories of a recent trip to Australia is the use of the phrase 'no worries' from all those who gave us excellent, efficient and 'laid-back' service.

We may worry because of the sin of self-reliance and self-effort. We may not have learnt how to enter God's rest, and instead may be striving in our own strength. We may be lacking wisdom and discernment about our situation. Yet God understands our needs and wants to lead us by the Spirit, so that others will recognise we are 'sons of God'. (See Romans 8:14.) Once we learn how to walk in the Spirit and to enter God's rest, the key is to stay there and to have confidence, *...that He who has begun a good work in you will complete it until the day of Jesus Christ* (Phil.1:6).

How do we walk not according to the flesh but according to the Spirit?

For those who live according to the flesh set their minds on the things of the flesh, but those who live according to the Spirit, the things of the Spirit.

For to be carnally minded is death, but to be spiritually minded is life and peace.

Because the carnal mind is enmity against God; for it is not subject to the law of God, nor indeed can it be.

So then, those who are in the flesh cannot please God.

But you are not in the flesh but in the Spirit, if indeed the Spirit of God dwells in you. Now if anyone does not have the Spirit of Christ, he is not His (Romans 8:5–10).

The key to success in the workplace is this focus. It is a great challenge, but we have at all times to seek to set our minds on the things of the Spirit. If we do this, we will not desire what belongs to the flesh. It is not a question of what we have to give up. Rather, it is concentrating on God's priorities—which we have to do afresh each day.

Entering God's rest is the alternative to worrying. In the letter to the Hebrews, the writer shows how to enter, and indicates in Chapters 3–4 what stopped the children of Israel from entering the Promised Land. God requires of us that we simply believe and obey Him. We do face temptations, tests and trials at work and it may be that our job is on the line. Jobs for life are no longer the norm. To overcome, we need to trust God and to make sure that, when we do not understand the circumstances, we do not then become embittered or get into rebellion. When I was baptised at the age of sixteen, a hymn was being sung as I came out of the water, which simply says it all: 'Trust and obey, for there is no other way to be happy in Jesus, but to trust and obey.'

God made man to live in His rest. When I started to share this, some years ago, it was a message that made the most dramatic impact on people's lives, whether in church, university or convention. God has prepared for our material and spiritual needs. The work has been completed, and for our part we must only obey God, trust and live for Him. God's Holy Spirit will help us and guide us into the things He has prepared for us. God prepares; He knows our situation, and can supply anything we need. His help is always well-timed, coming just when we need it. (See Heb. 4:16.)

Jesus tells us not to worry about the material things of life: clothing, and what we eat and drink. He uses the illustration of the birds flying around and says that His Father knows each of them and feeds them. *Are you not of more value than they?* (Matt 6:26). Of course we are; and Jesus is saying that we can forget the basic necessities, which God knows we have need of, and start exercising faith by seeking first the kingdom of God and His righteousness. Peter tells us how to deal with anxiety, by: *casting all your care upon Him, for He cares for you* (1 Peter 5:7). This is an action of the will, and if we are in a tough work situation it is something we have to repeat until we finally let go. It may be that we have to repent of the sin of self-reliance and self-effort.

The key to our daily needs being met is to— *Seek first the kingdom of God and His righteousness, and all these things shall be* [not may be] *added to you* (Matt 6:33). Jesus concludes with a great piece of advice. *Therefore do not worry about tomorrow, for tomorrow will worry about its own things. Sufficient for the day is its own trouble* (Matt. 6:34). This is not easy when you prepare your business plan and SWOT analysis. But my wife always tells me to take things a day at a time—and, as usual, she is right. Don't fear for the future. God has provided for it, and He is our supply. Do not worry!

10. DO NOT JUDGE

Matthew 7:1–6

Judge not, that you be not judged. For with what judgment you judge, you will be judged; and with the measure you use, it will be measured back to you (Matt. 7:1). Does this mean that output measurement, benchmarking and performance appraisal are wrong for Christians —or that we cannot judge performance and, where necessary, take disciplinary action or obtain proper legal redress? The answer is 'no'. The term'judge' is being used here in the sense of 'condemn', or 'pass final judgment', and that belongs only to God.

> 'It is mine to avenge,' says God (Rom. 12:19). 'Judge nothing before the time,' says Paul. God is the searcher of hearts. 'He—and he alone—is capable of fully assessing genuineness and integrity. Our opinions are at best provisional.' (Michael Eaton).

Matthew 7:1 is one of the most misquoted passages of Scripture, often being misunderstood through being taken out of context. The state has a God-given responsibility to administer sound justice. Parents and church leaders have responsibilities, which require sound judgment and corresponding actions, as do employers and those with management and supervisory responsibility. What Jesus is speaking of is *attitude*. Christians should not have a harsh and hyper-critical attitude toward others. When such negativity pervades the workplace, it often results in a blame culture. Sadly, this can also come into the life of a church, creating fear and stifling spiritual growth.

I thank God for my evangelical heritage and the emphasis on truth and 'the word'. But, sadly, it made me judgmental of others, and I had to be brought to a place of repentance so that God could baptise me with the Spirit, and show me that healing and the gifts of the Spirit are for today. After eighteen years of hyperactive Christianity, that was hard! What characterises our attitude toward people and situations at work—mercy and forgiveness, or judgementalism and the desire to punish? We are a forgiven people and, surely this should determine our approach. *For judgment is without mercy to the one who has shown no mercy. Mercy triumphs over judgment* (Jas. 2:13).

A task I often perform as a consultant is to produce an independent report, analysing particular problems in an organisation. Why did things go wrong? Why was there a failure? I always try to be objective, and to honestly interpret the information given to me in writing or through interviews. One of the reasons we should be slow to judge is that we rarely have the full picture, and inevitably bring our own preconceived ideas and even prejudices. My endeavour is always to try to be positive and to treat it as a learning experience for the organisation, as well as producing a plan, if necessary, for corrective action. I do not set out looking for scapegoats.

On this issue, the Gospel of Luke tells us more than we find in Matthew's account of the Sermon on the Mount:

Judge not, and you shall not be judged. Condemn not, and you shall not be condemned. Forgive, and you will be forgiven.

Give, and it will be given to you: good measure, pressed down, shaken together, and running over will be put into your bosom. For with the same measure that you use, it will be measured back to you (Luke 6:37–38).

Bringing the two together brings out the negative and positive sides of sowing and reaping. Whatever we sow, that is what we shall reap. If we sow patience, we shall reap patience; if we sow mercy, we shall reap mercy; if we sow forgiveness we shall reap forgiveness; if we sow generosity, we shall reap generosity; if we sow rejoicing, we shall reap joy; but similarly if we sow bitterness, we shall reap bitterness and destruction; if we sow unforgiveness, we shall reap torment.

When people treat us badly at work, we have a choice as how to respond. We can seek vengeance or we can seek God's blessing upon them. The world's way is to seek revenge. God's way is different— *Bless those who persecute you; bless and do not curse.... Repay no one evil for evil* (Romans 12:14,17), and, *Do not be overcome by evil but overcome evil with good* (v. 21). This is our best safeguard against hypocrisy (i.e. seeing the faults in others and not in ourselves.) A practical help can be having the right mentor, who can help us not to turn our 'splinters' into 'planks'.

Are God's ways easy? No; not in my experience. Do they work? Yes —always, and often in the most dramatic ways, beginning firstly with me. If we have been judgmental and critical as known Christians in the workplace, we then find that this law of 'reciprocity' comes into play, as it surely must. Our sound statements of faith and attempts at effective witness will seem like pearls having been cast before swine, and the result is that our witness is torn to pieces. We should be those who look for the good in people, avoid hypocrisy, have a trusted mentor who will tell us our faults, and continually ask God for help.

11. THE GOLDEN RULE

Matthew 7:7– 23

Ask, and it will be given to you; seek, and you will find; knock, and it will be opened to you. For everyone who asks receives, and he who seeks finds, and to him who knocks it will be opened (Matt. 7:7–8).
Does God get tired of our work problems? —Certainly not! We discover for ourselves the truth that He is interested in every detail of our working life, once we recognise that work is our calling, and that we really can ask for His help. What is needed to gain the confidence to ask is to get an understanding of His will. Once we know this, we can then ask with confidence, and with the expectation that we *will* receive. We can, for example, always ask with confidence for wisdom, because God has promised to give it generously, as long as we are not double-minded. (See James 1:5.) Answers do not always come as quickly as we expect, and we need to be persistent. One of the reasons may be that we are not ready to receive. God knows what is best for us, and His timing is always perfect. Praying for a dynamic young(er) Christian leader earlier this year, I had that sense that God was about to answer his prayers. He has! I will not say what it was about; but the person concerned will not be leading the singles' week at Spring Harvest this year! God understands corporate plans, succession planning, time management and emotional intelligence. He knows the issues on which we should be concentrating and specialises in crisis management. Ask Him! He promises only to give good things.

Therefore, whatever you want men to do to you, do also to them, for this is the Law and the Prophets (Matt. 7:12).
This is often called the Golden Rule, and it would have been a good strap line for our customer care programme at work. Did we treat people who came to the office (or telephoned) in the way we ourselves would wish to be treated? Were we open, honest and responsive? We had a great team but were even better when we thought these

things through. The same sort of thinking should happen in church, where, we are told, 70% of visitors return not because of the preaching, but because of the welcome they receive. If members of the public insisted on seeing the Chief Executive, then I would see them, sometimes with unexpected results. James calls this teaching 'the royal law'. (See James 2:8.)

We are on a narrow way, but we are not called to be narrow, boring people. In *Being Unmistakably Christian at Work*, I describe a work style that will cause us to stand out from the crowd. We have to keep doing good; refusing to compromise without becoming religious and boring. We have abundant life, and the challenge is to live that out in the workplace. It is tough at times, yet always exciting. Being surrounded by friends and colleagues who face 'destruction' motivates me to pray that my life will demonstrate the fruit of the Spirit, and that I should be able to move constantly in the power of the Spirit. When I was going through a challenging time at work, a Bishop friend came to the office to pray for me. My secretary told me, after she became a Christian, that when the Bishop, who was travelling incognito, (i.e. he had a tie and was smiling) went through her room, she felt a presence. That, praise God, was the anointing. A dynamic senior woman manager I was mentoring said to me after a few months, 'I have come to the conclusion there is someone who watches over you.' Our lives should create a hunger in others, which can only be satisfied by meeting Jesus—the preacher of the Sermon on the Mount.

The spirit of the end times is deception, and we need to be on our guard. We test what we hear against the word of God. We also need discernment, to test whether manifestations are truly signs of God's blessing. But let us be open, taking care how we judge (see Chapter 10) knowing that the ultimate test is the fruit. In almost every case that I have prayed for sick colleagues to be healed, it has led to them becoming Christians. That is the most important fruit I want to see. Do we have false prophets in the workplace? Yes—there can be prophets of doom and gloom, and others who are driven by fear or greed. We can be prophetic in the workplace, and we can learn to test all things. God may speak prophetically to warn, encourage and give direction about our jobs and businesses. The people God uses may not even realise they are being prophetic, but we know when we have heard the truth.

It was said to me recently that only someone that you trust can deceive you, and I was shocked by the simple truth of the statement. The test is this: are they doing the will of the Father? The workplace can be a very fulfilling place for the Christian who is aware of his/her calling, but it is also a battleground, so we need to be alert, and continually on our guard.

12. ESTABLISH RIGHT FOUNDATIONS

Matthew 7:24–29

The wise man built his house upon the rock. I can still remember the Sunday school chorus —and the actions of building hand upon hand, followed by a loud clap, to signal the fall of the house built on the sand as it fell, due to wind and floods. What makes the difference? The answer is found in verse 24:

Therefore whoever hears these sayings of Mine, ***and does them****, I will liken him to a wise man who built his house on the rock.*

The rock is the teaching of Jesus; and wisdom is to take appropriate action. **The solid foundation for our life is the word of God**. When the temptations, tests and trials come (the storms and the floods) then the strength of our foundations will be revealed. Jesus said that those who hear His words and act on them build wisely.

So what is our **Action Plan**, for applying the Sermon on the Mount to the workplace? My suggestions are that, as we put our relationship with Him and His word first in our lives, we should determine —

☑ To be merciful, pure in heart, a peacemaker, teachable and open to the Holy Spirit;
☑ To be salt and light; and to do works that glorify God;
☑ To be positive, seek reconciliation, keep right relationships and do what is righteous;
☑ To keep our word, be honest, and think before we speak;
☑ To do more than the minimum, give our best and speak blessings over our enemies;

☑ To do good deeds knowing that we shall be judged by our actions;
☑ To start the day with prayer and to pray for our work, employers and colleagues;
☑ To tithe, and to give over and above to the poor and to 'the gospel', as directed by the Holy Spirit;
☑ To give up worry and anxiety, and to recognise that God is our supply;
☑ To look for the good in people, avoid hypocrisy, and ask God for help;
☑ To look for and develop the best in others;
☑ To spend quality time in the word and put it into practice in our lives.

What was the reaction to Jesus' teaching?

And so it was, when Jesus had ended these sayings, that the people were astonished at His teaching, for He taught them as one having authority, and not as the scribes (Matt. 7:28–29).

The Sermon on the Mount offers God's blueprint for Christian behaviour in the workplace. There is no better, more definitive or authoritative guidance available. Each of us has to decide how we are going to respond. The challenge is great, but we are promised by God the resources to succeed. All we need to do is to ask Him.